30 Days of Arizona
SUNSETS

Errol Jud Coder

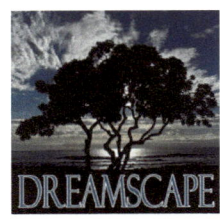

Photographed by by Errol Jud Coder
Cover design by Errol Jud Coder
Cover photo: Sunset looking west towards Phoenix, Arizona.

Books by Dreamscape Publishing are available at a special bulk discount for promotional and commercial use.
Visit www.dreamscapepublishing.webs.com

Printed in the United States
10 9 8 7 6 5 4 3 2 1
ISBN-13: 978-1496023636
ISBN-10: 1496023633

NOTE Every effort has been taken to ensure that all information in this book is correct and accurate. Any identified errors and needed corrections, as well as additions will be added to future editions.

Clouds come floating into my life, no longer to carry rain or usher storm, but to add color to my sunset sky.

-Rabindranath Tagore

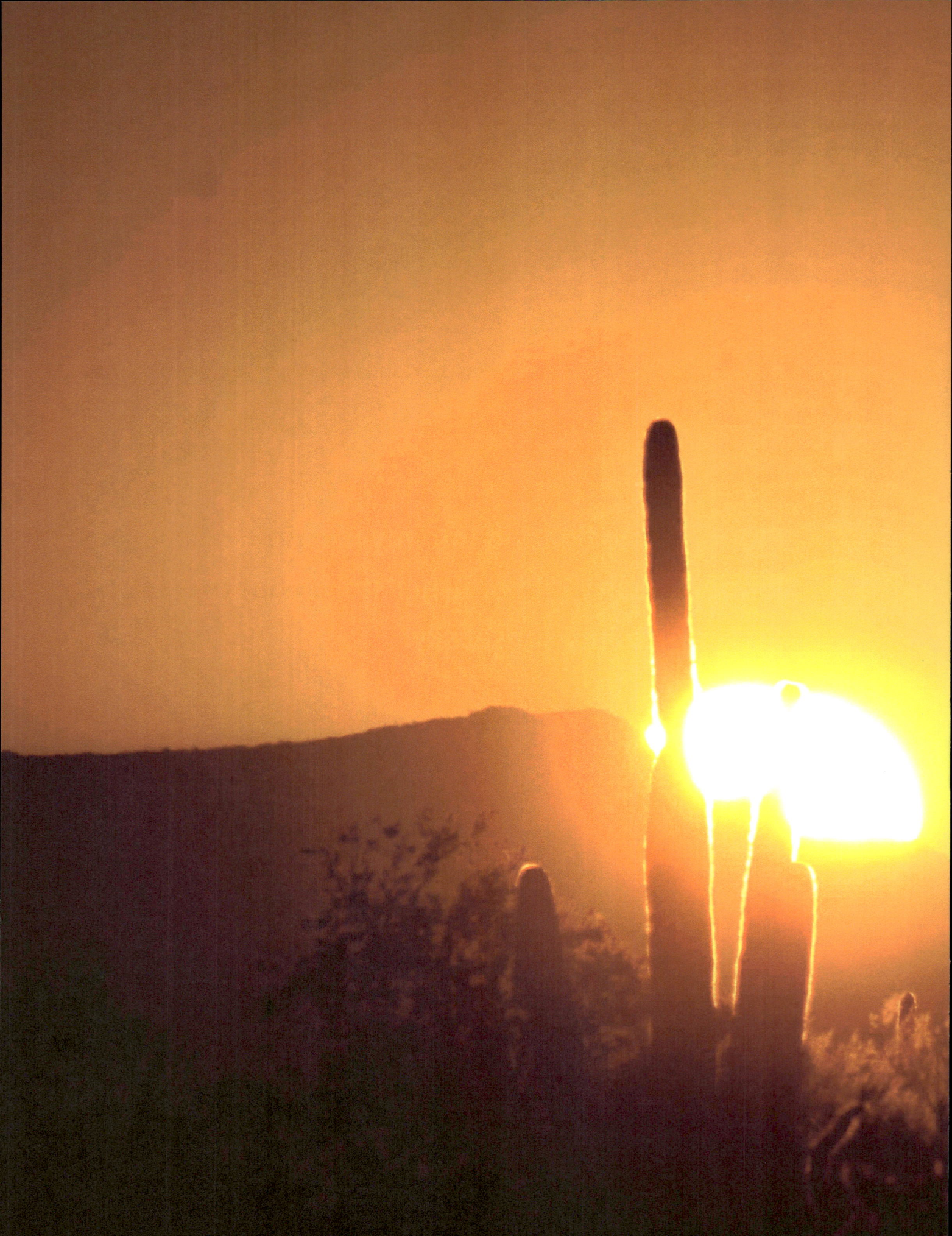

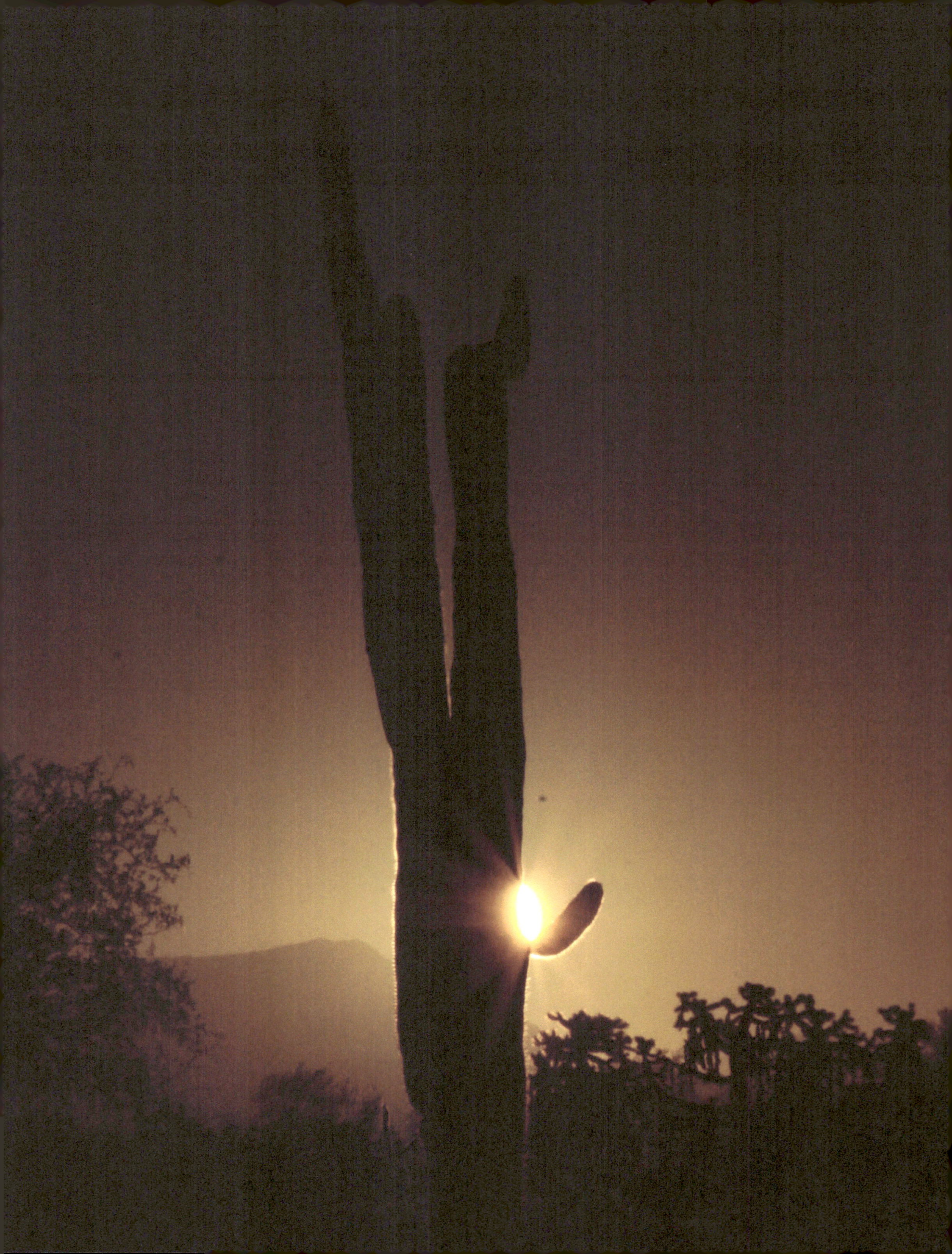

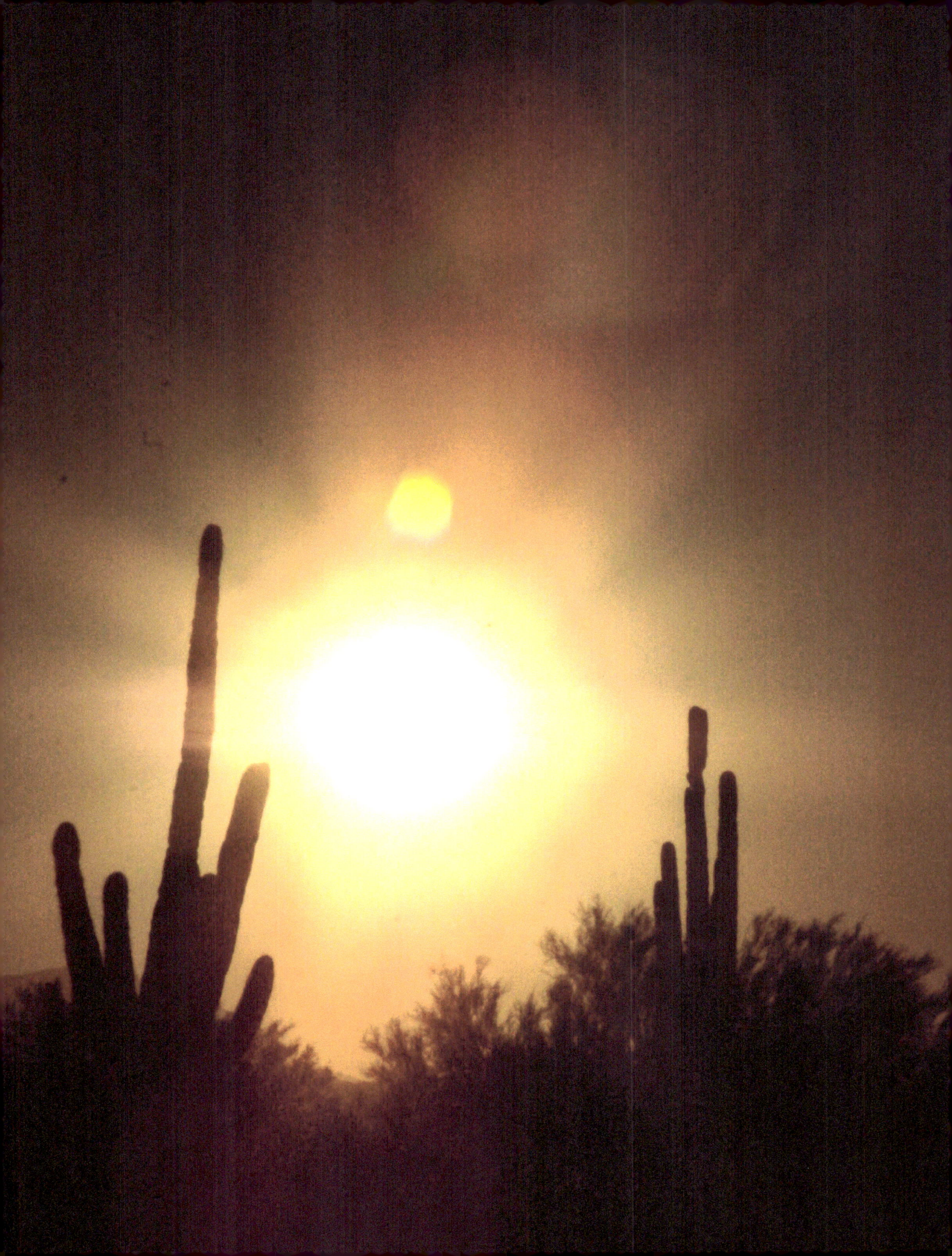

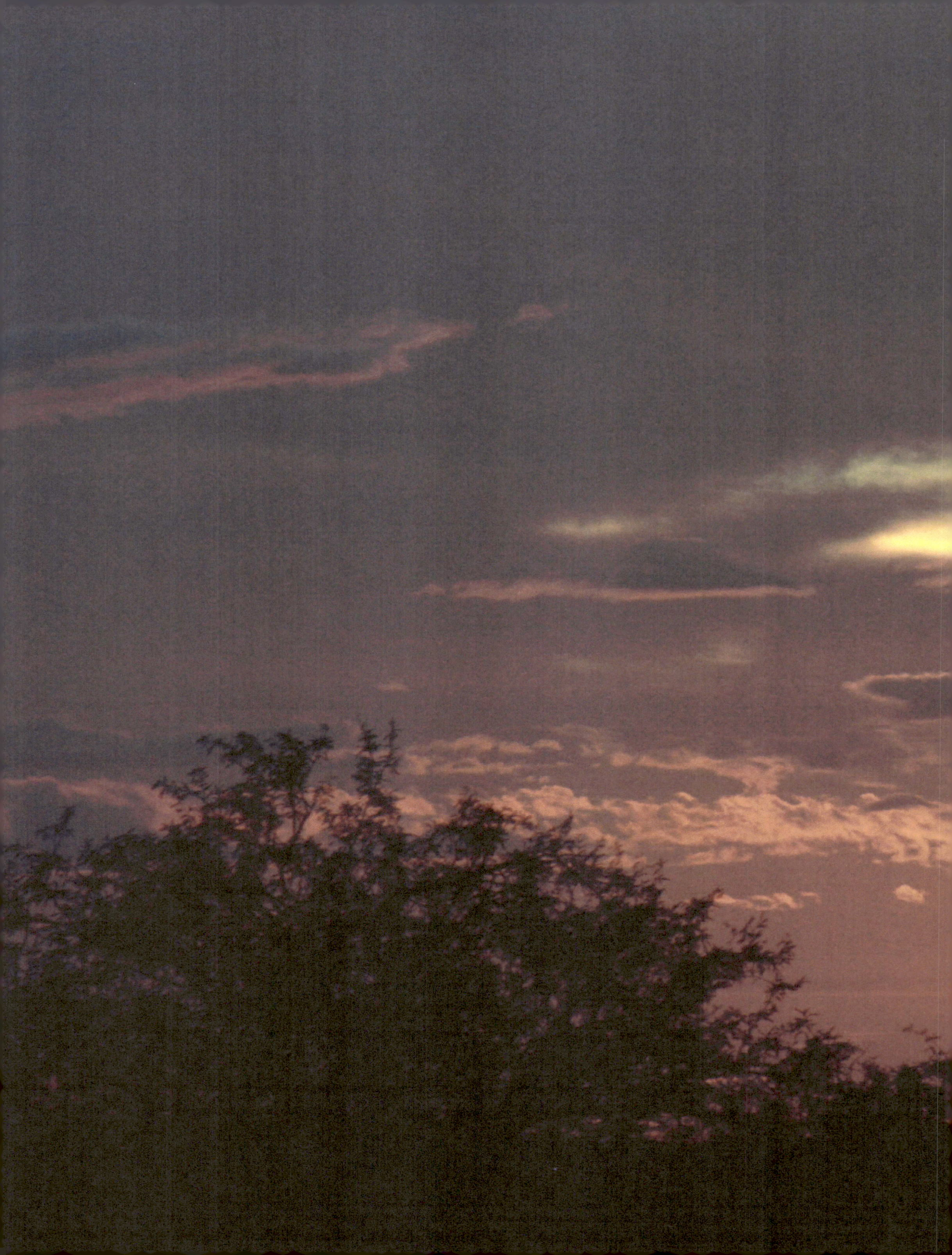

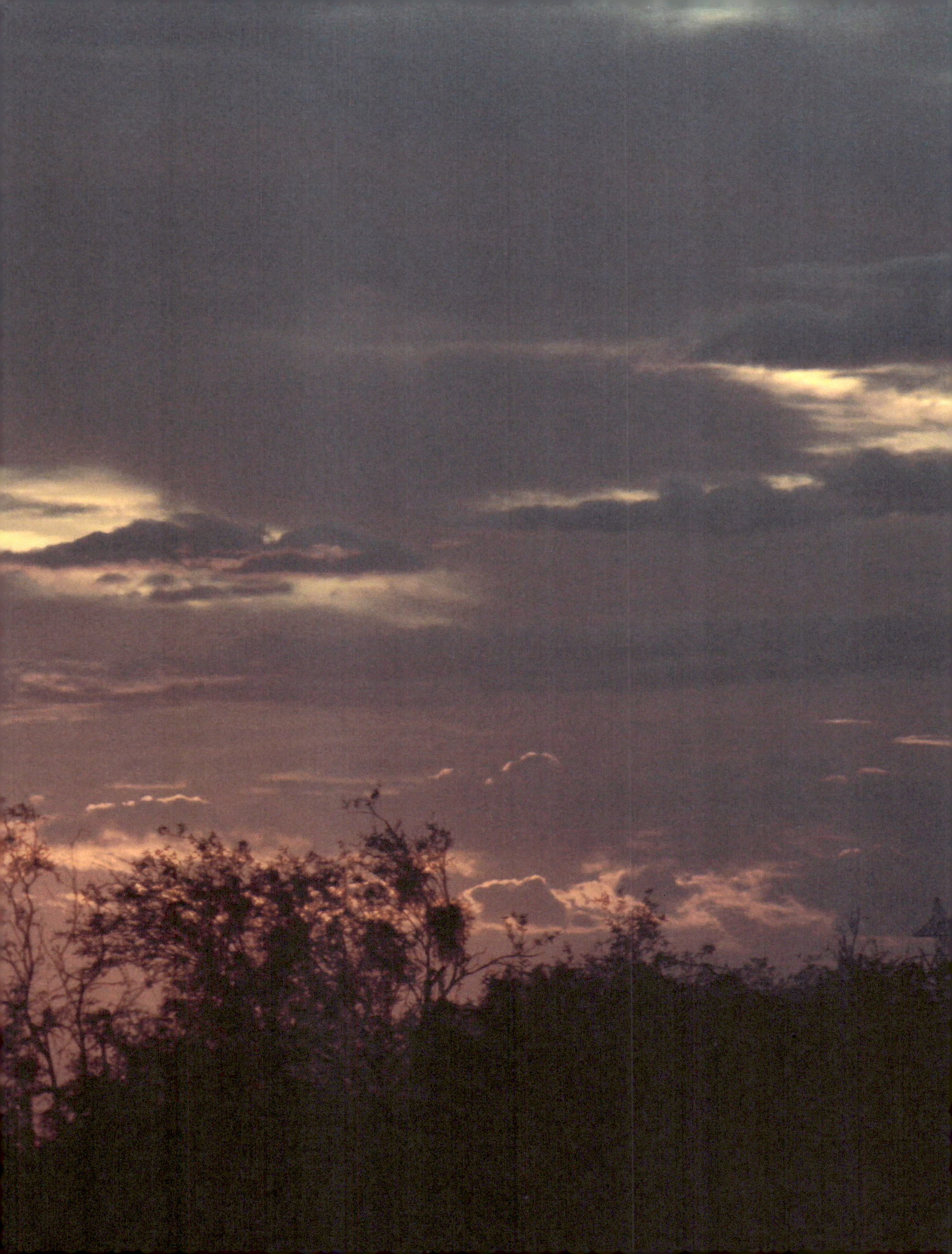

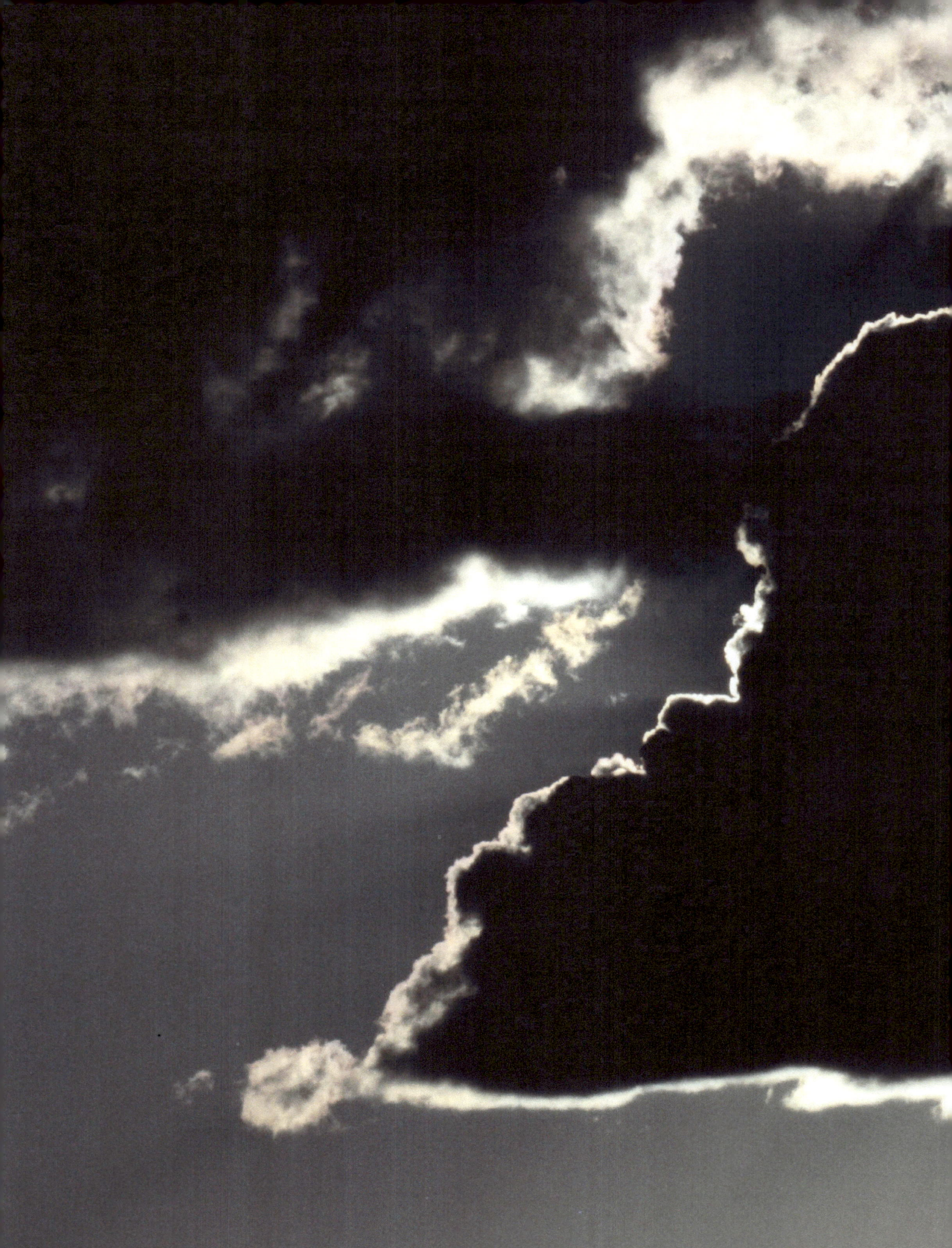

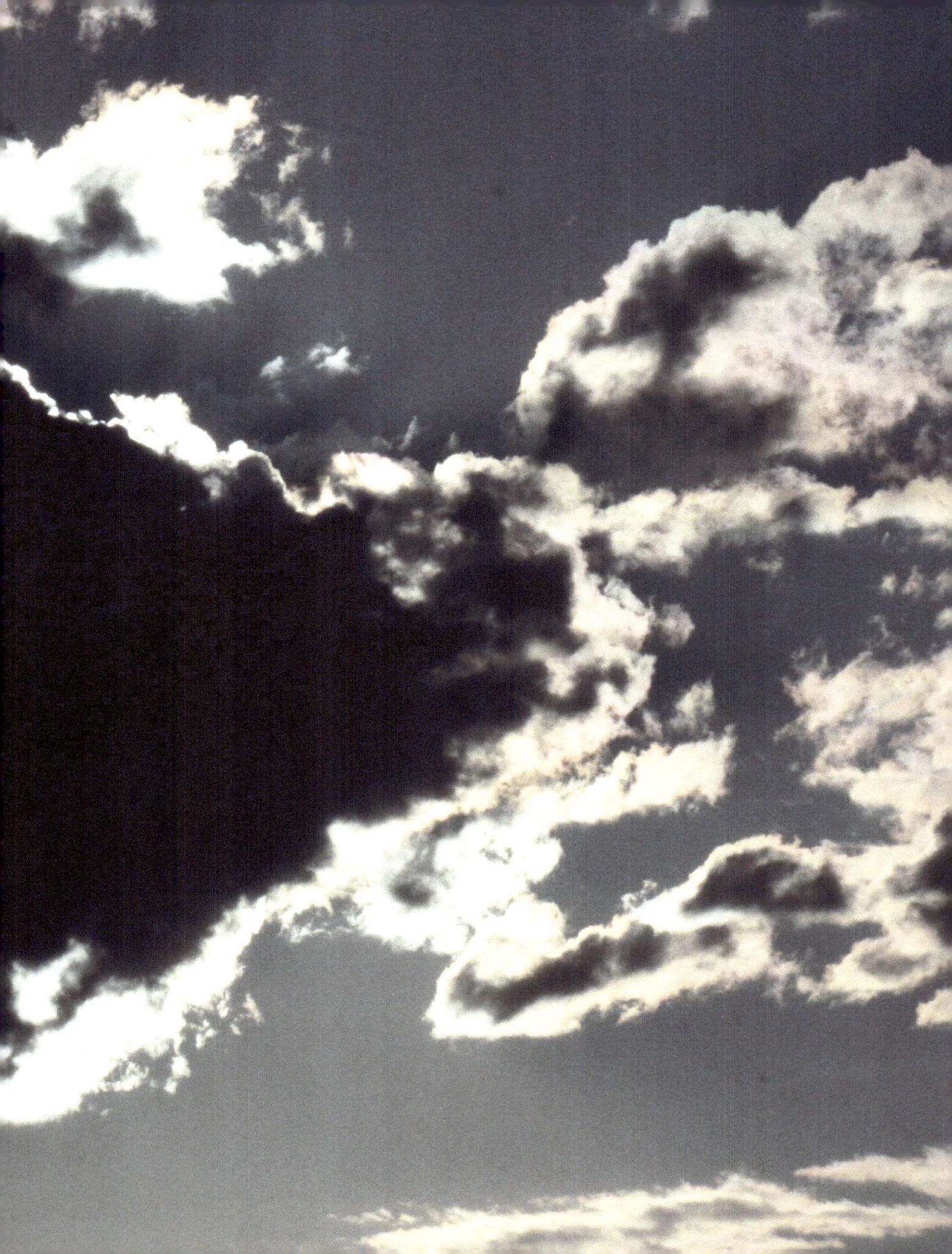

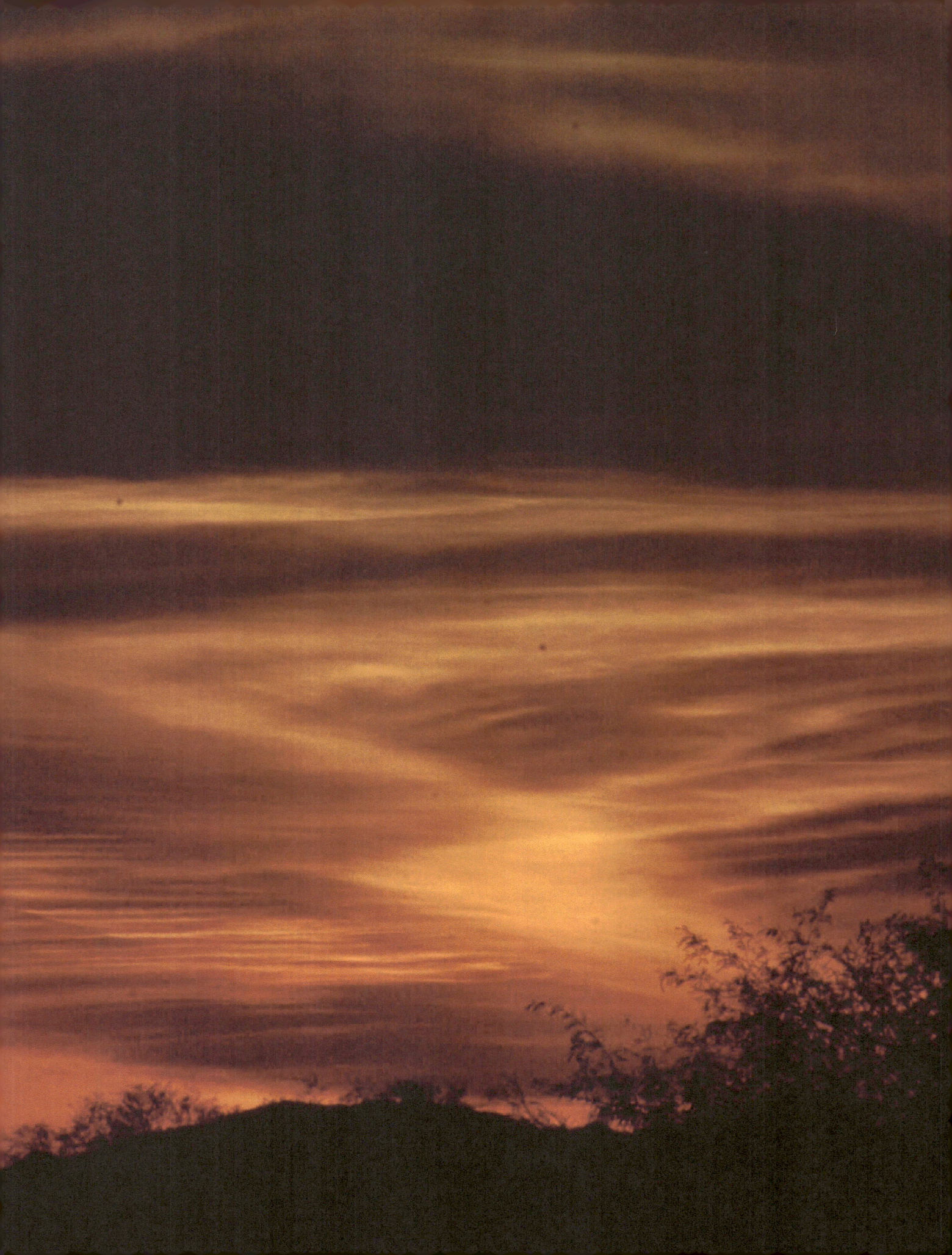

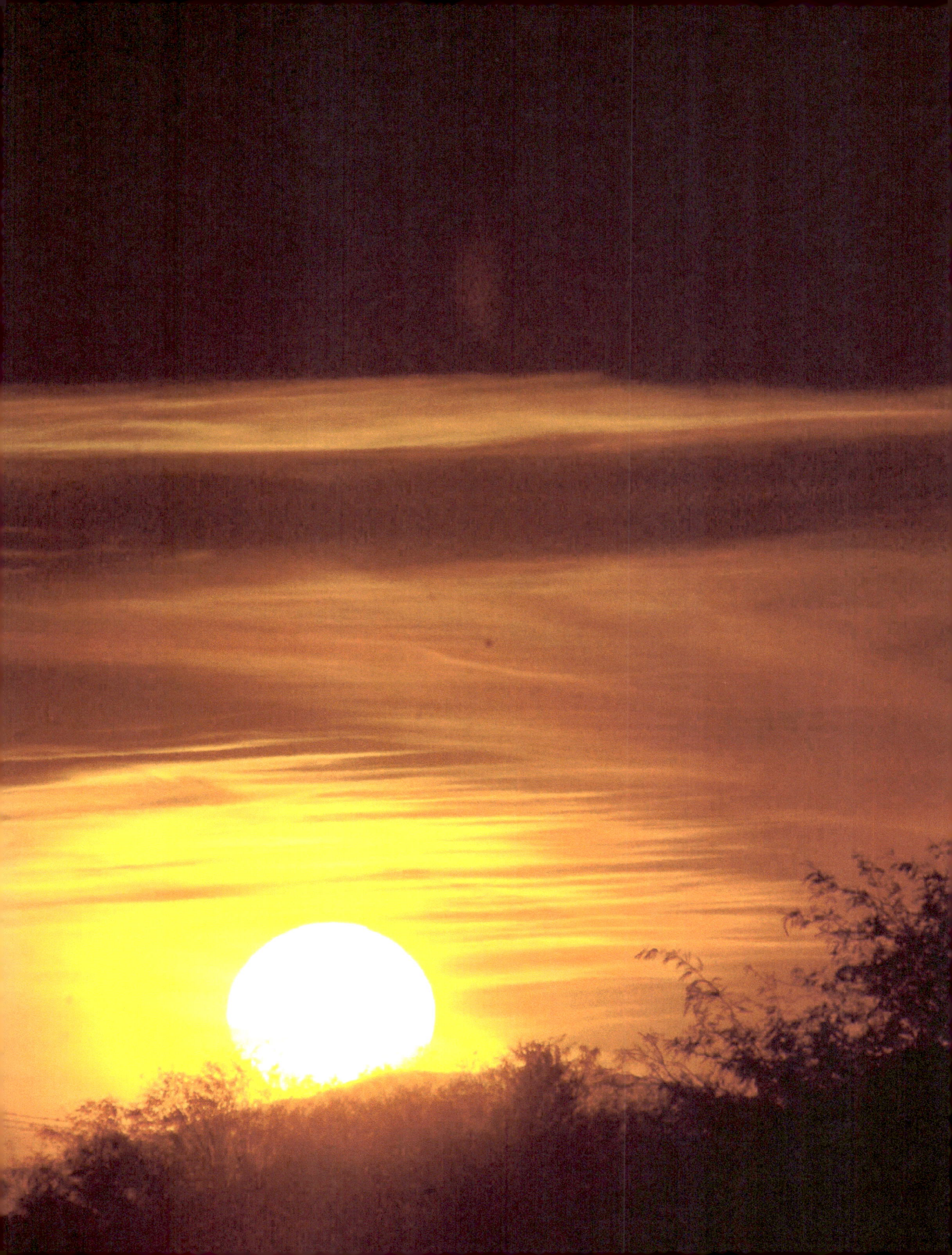

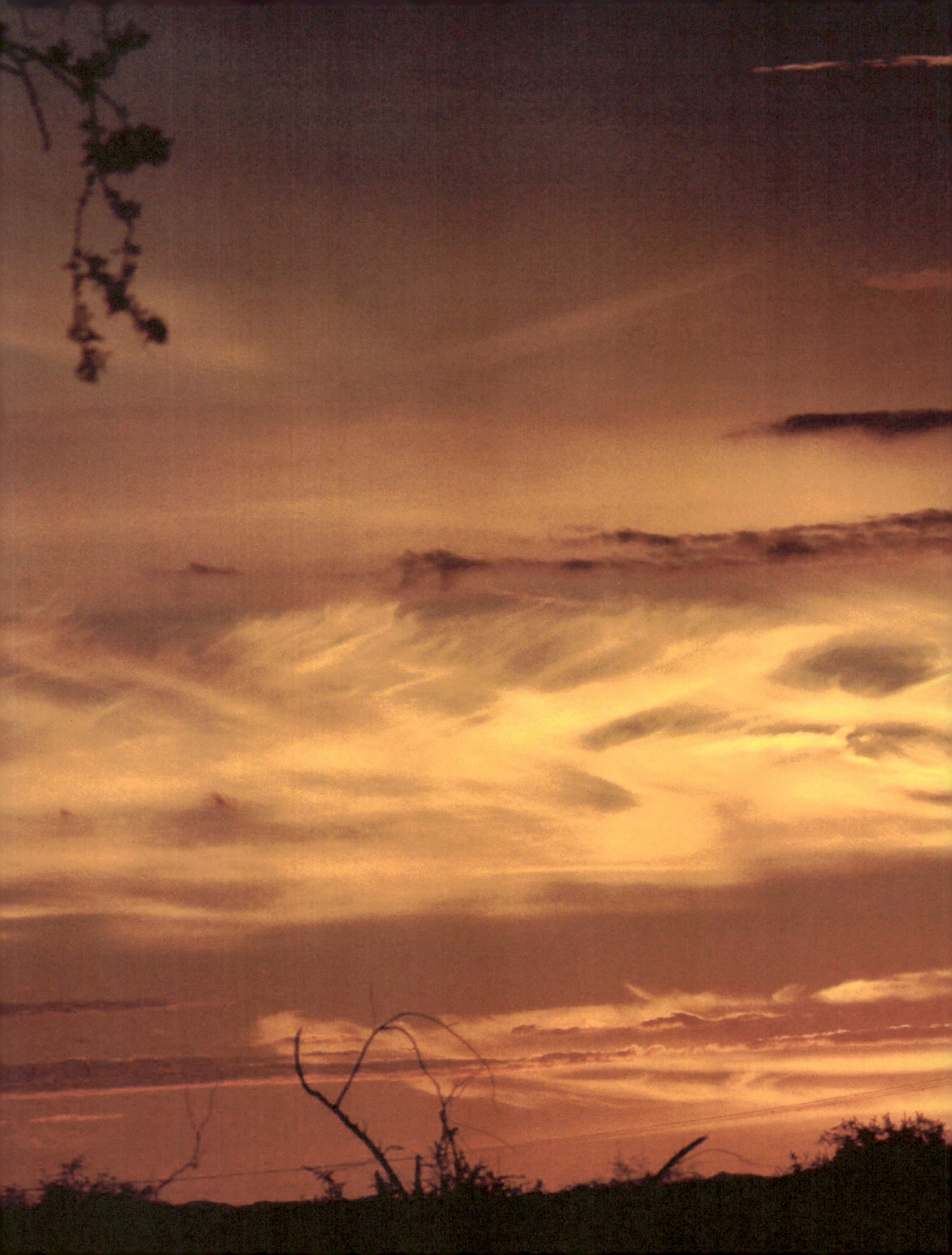

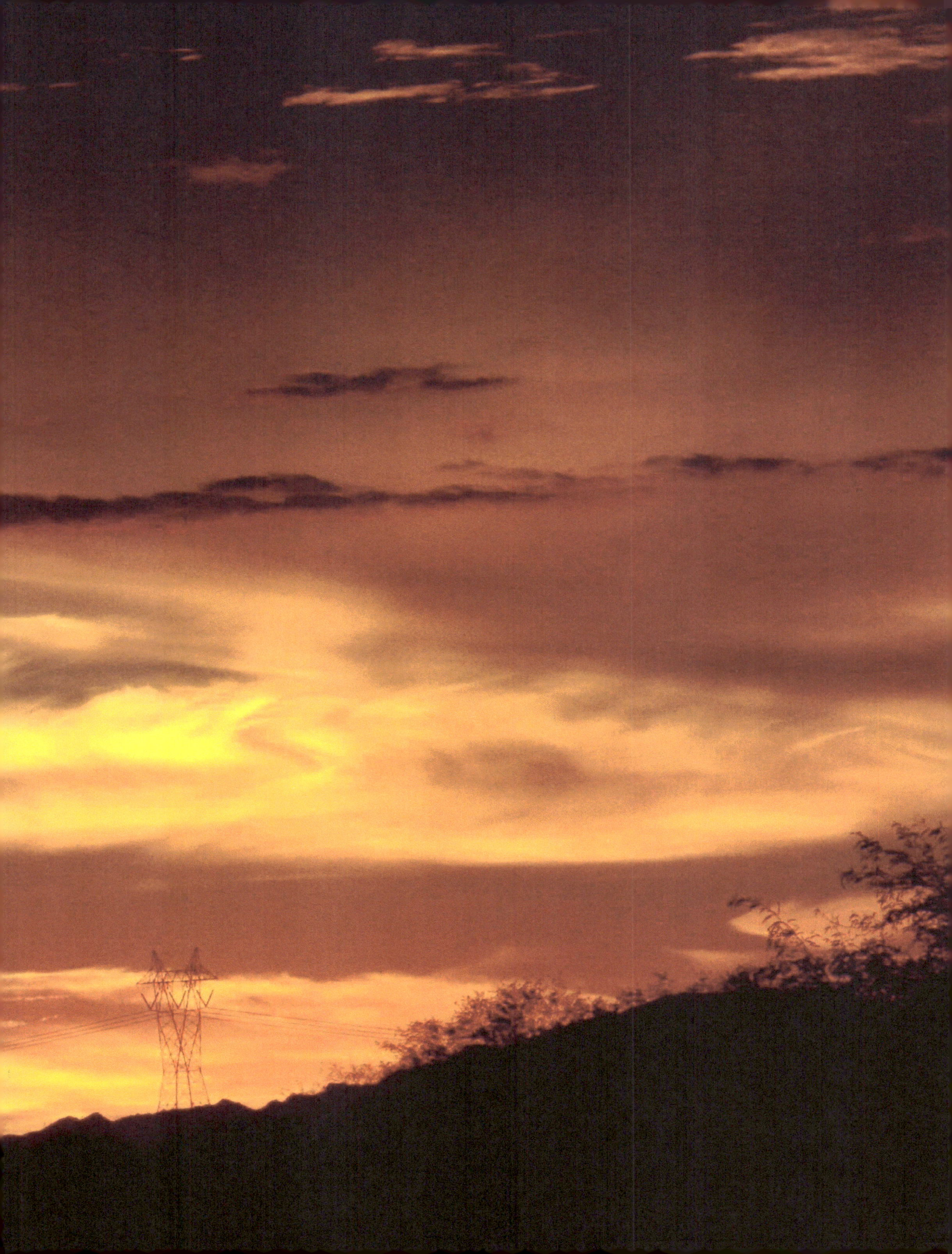

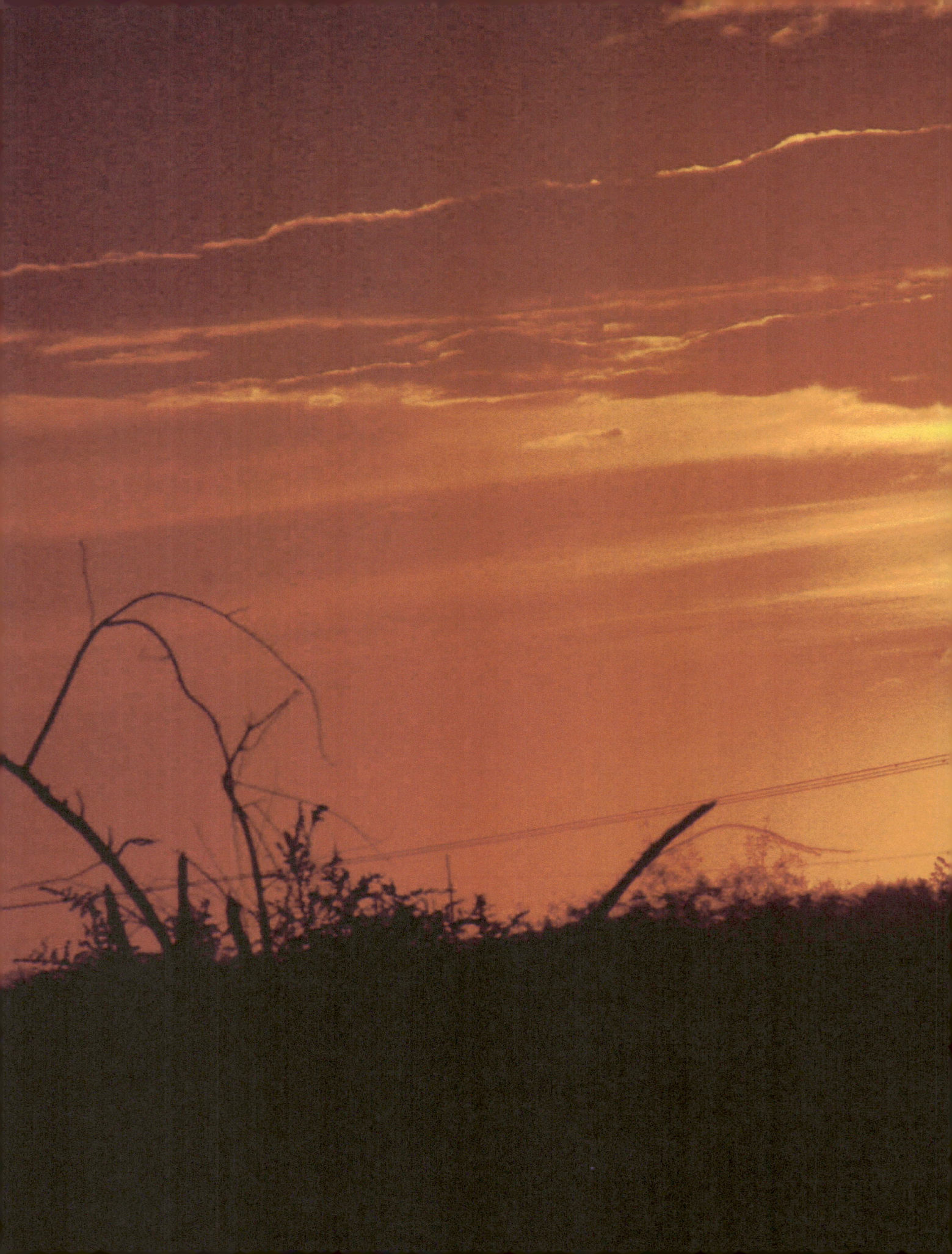

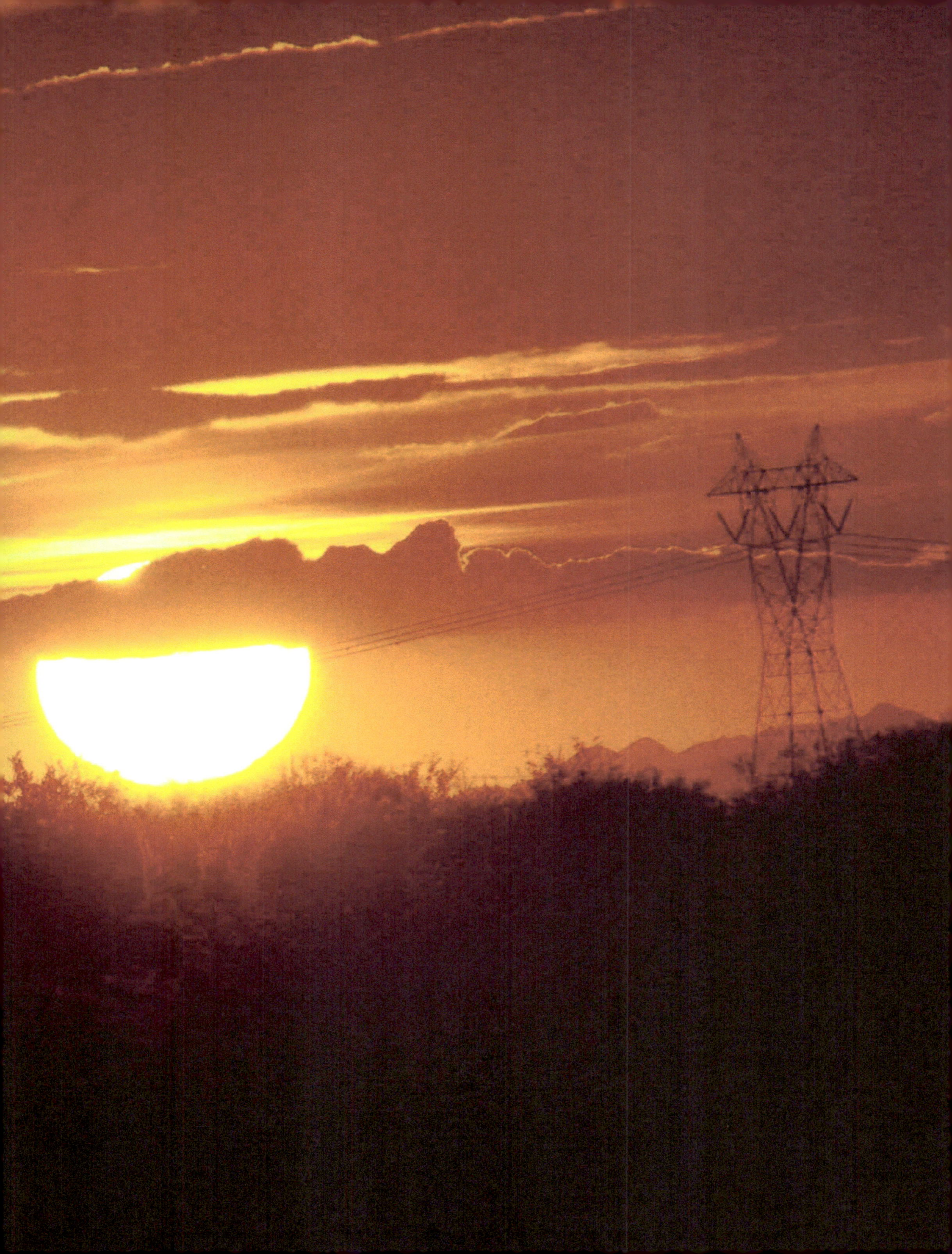

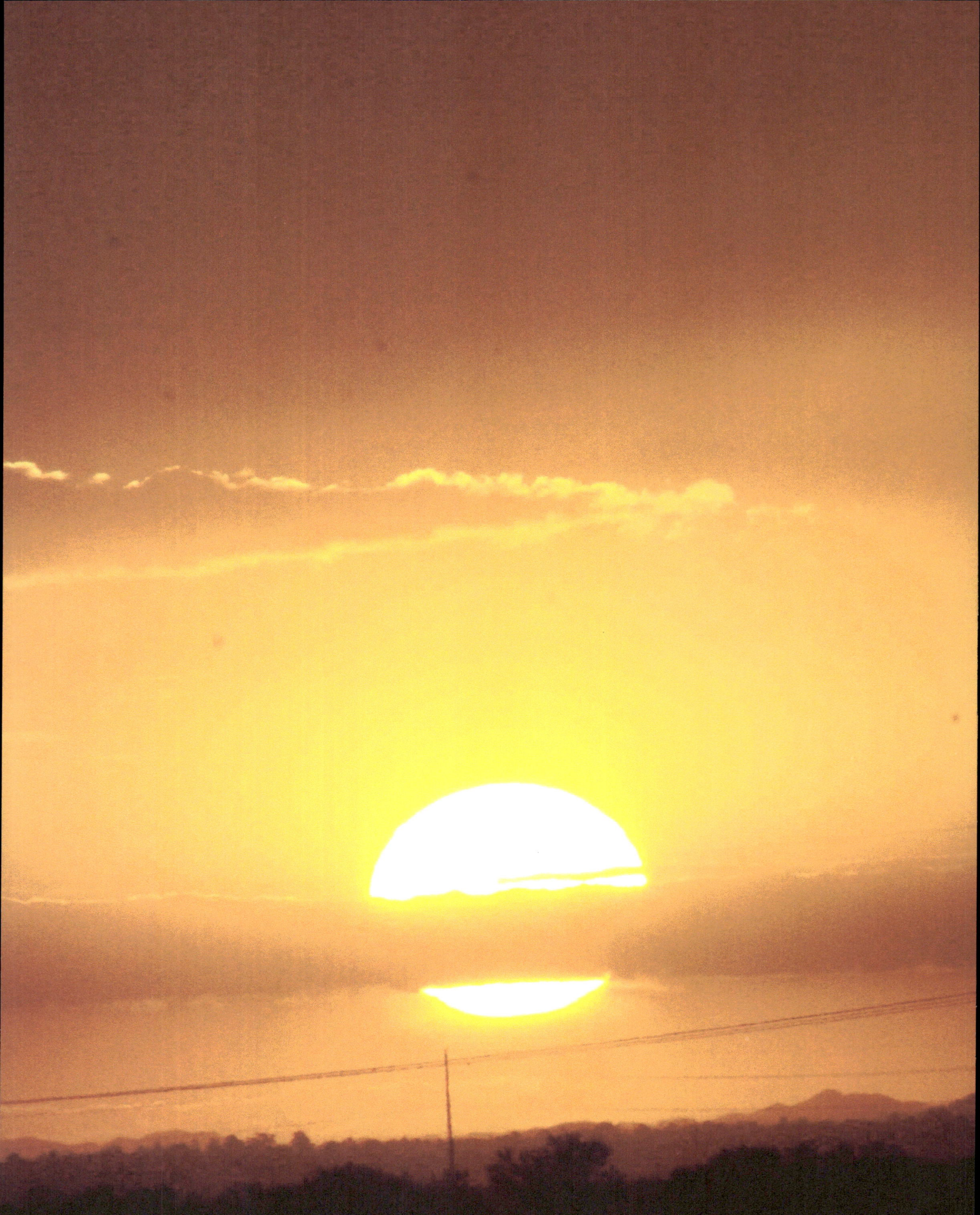

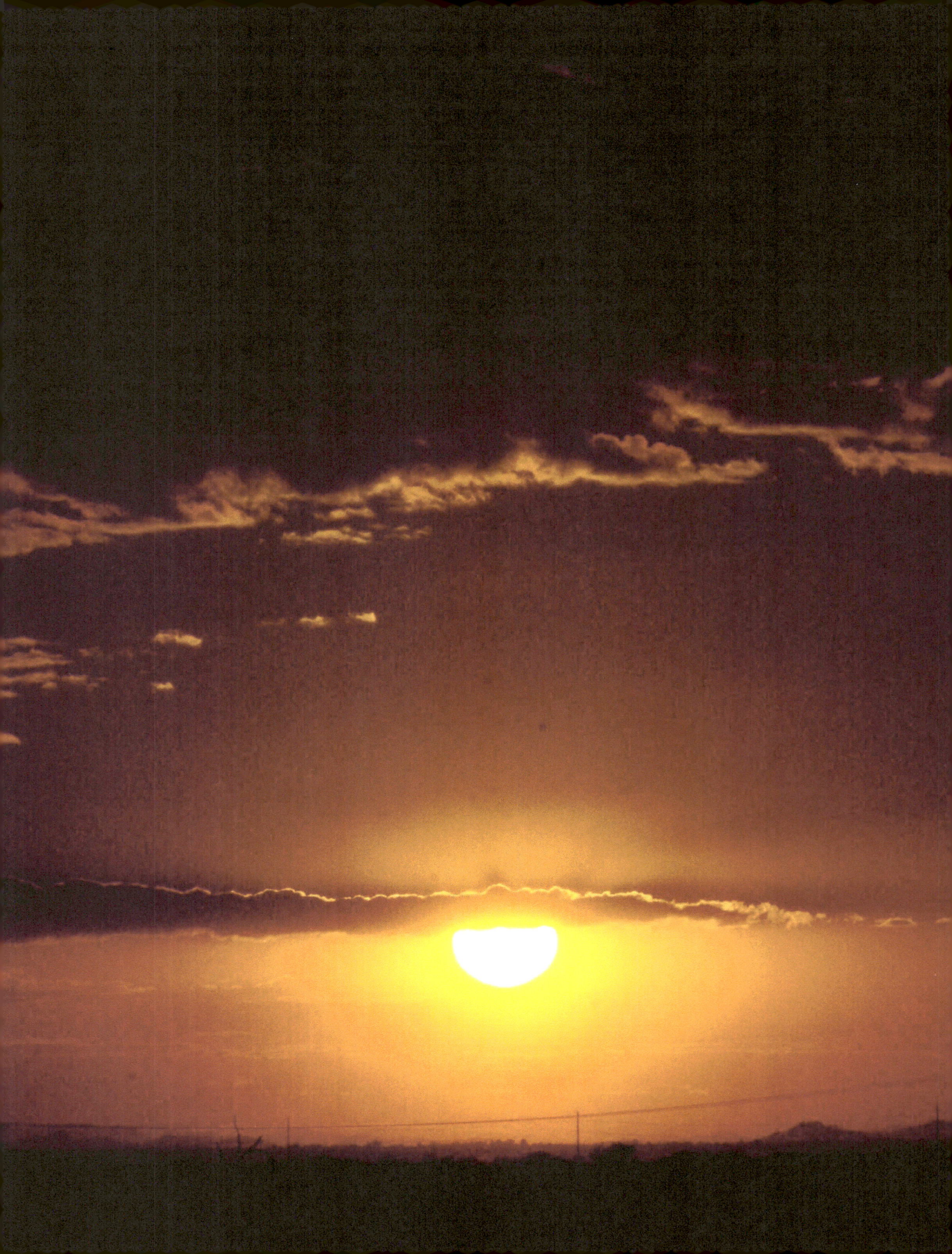

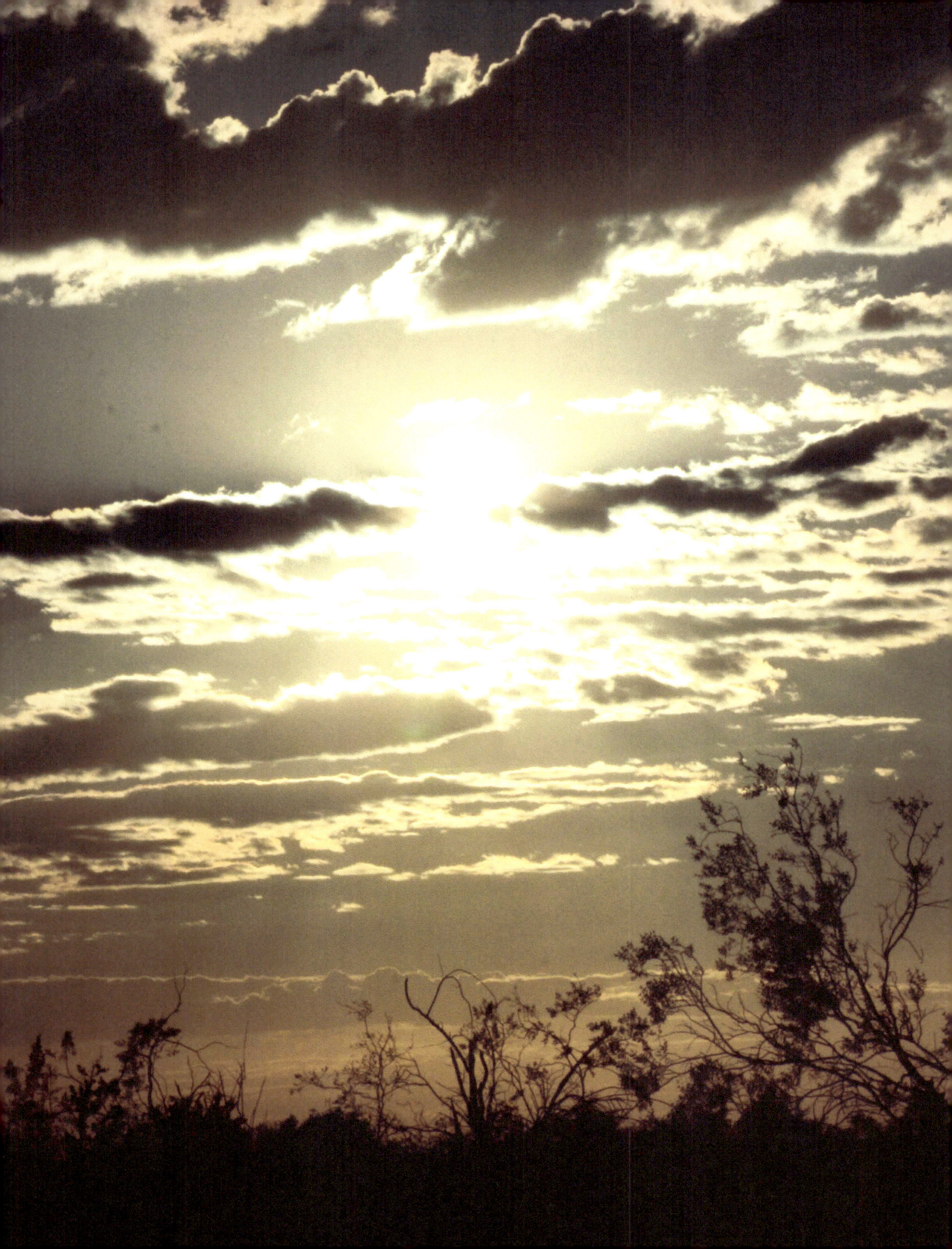

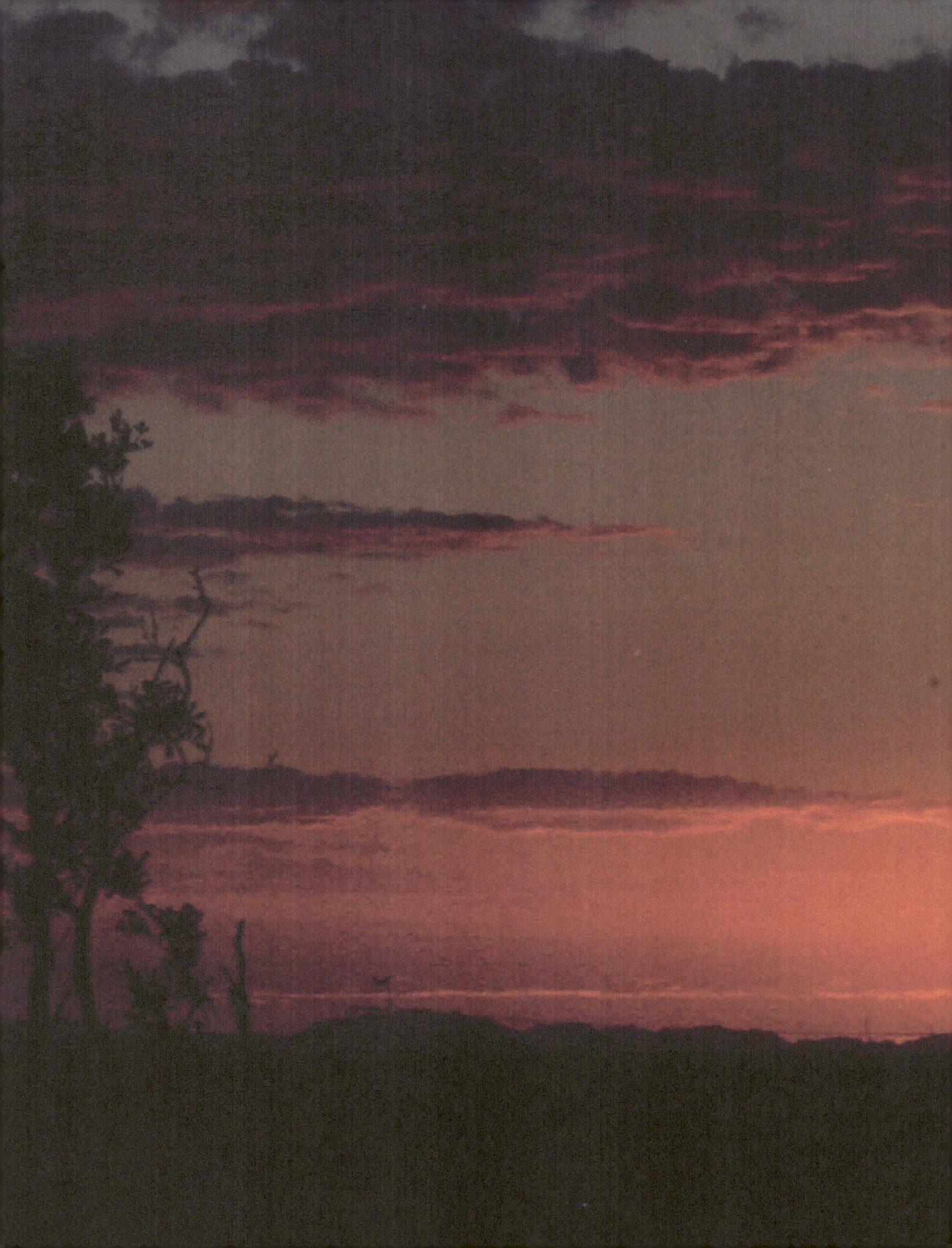

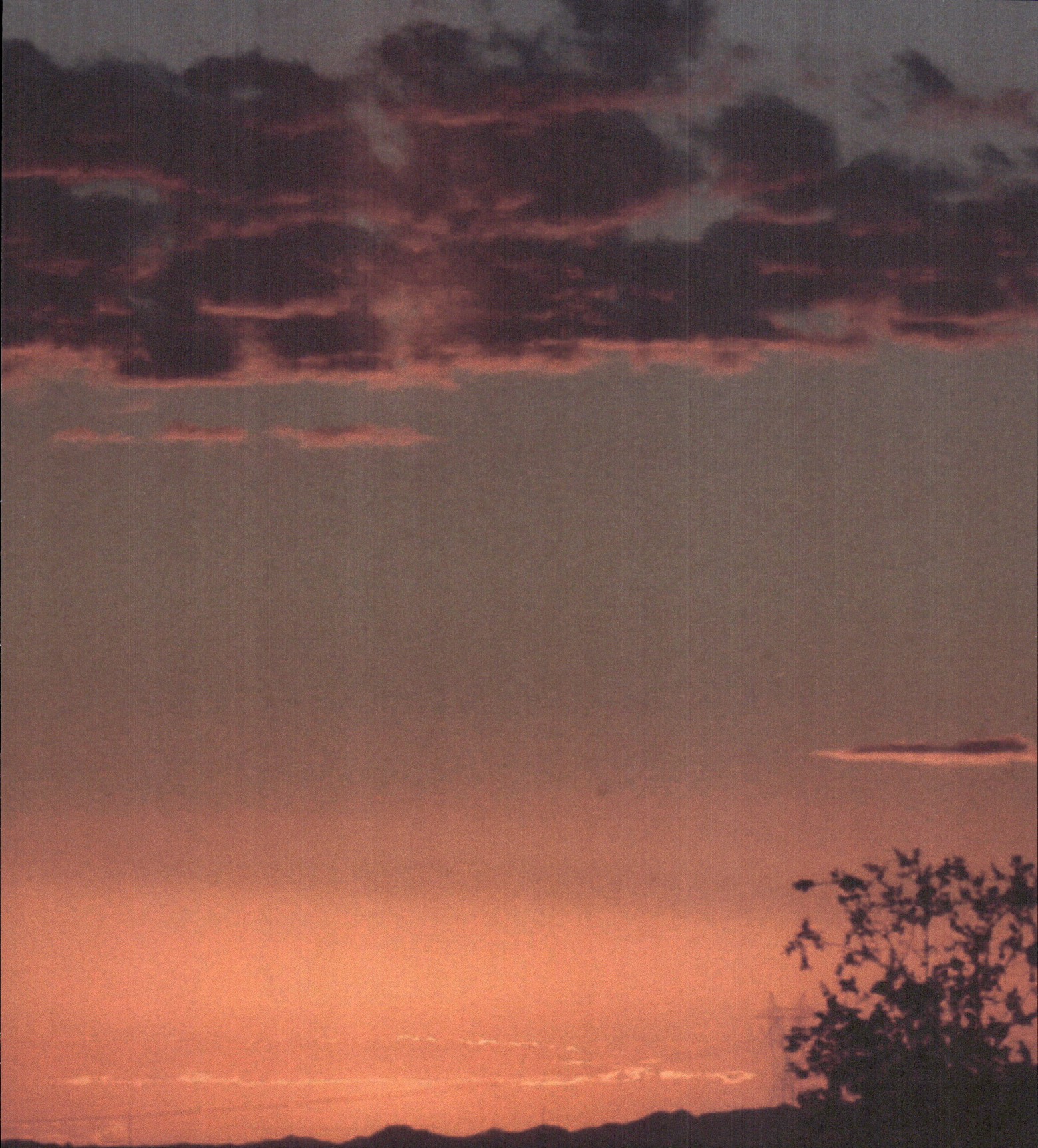

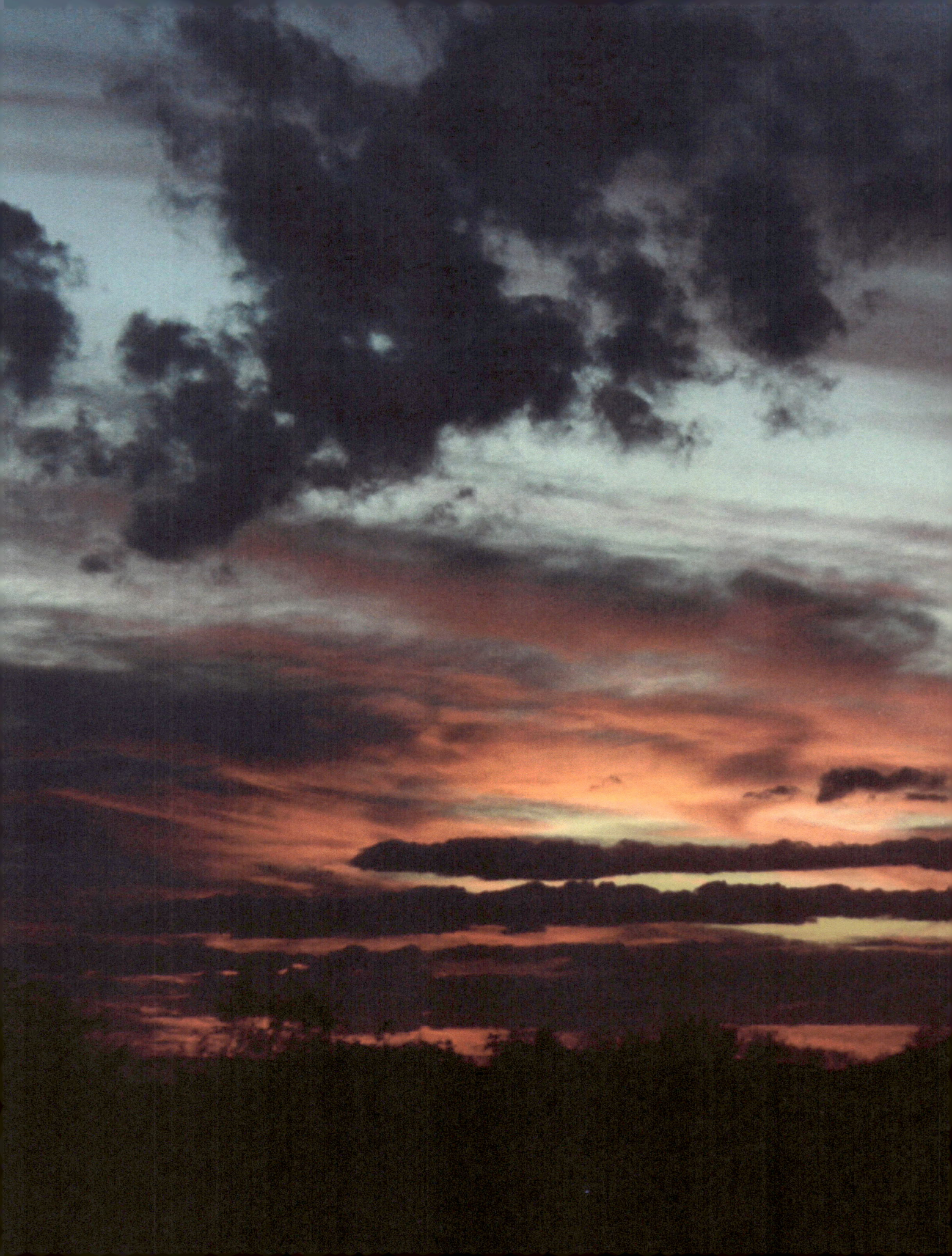

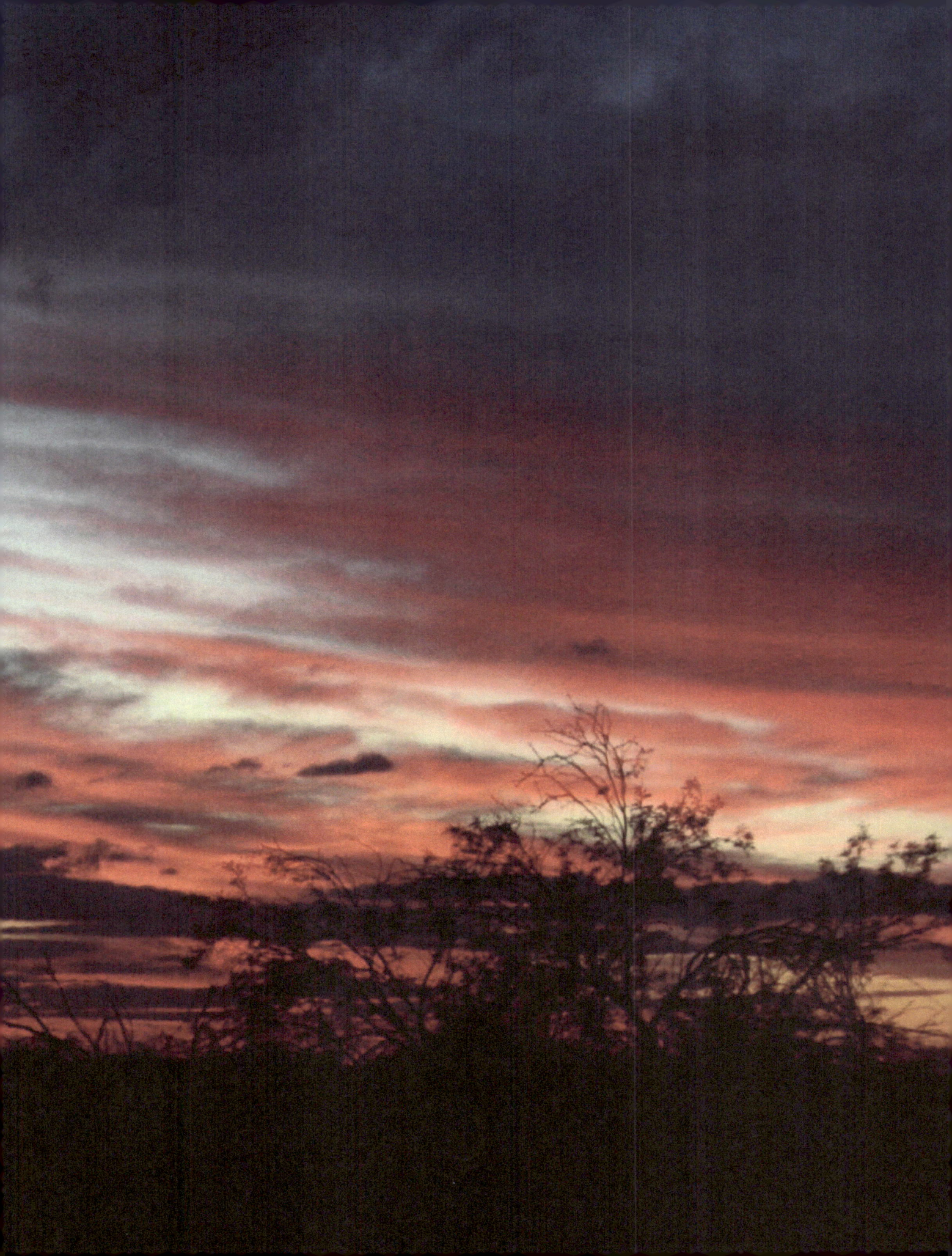

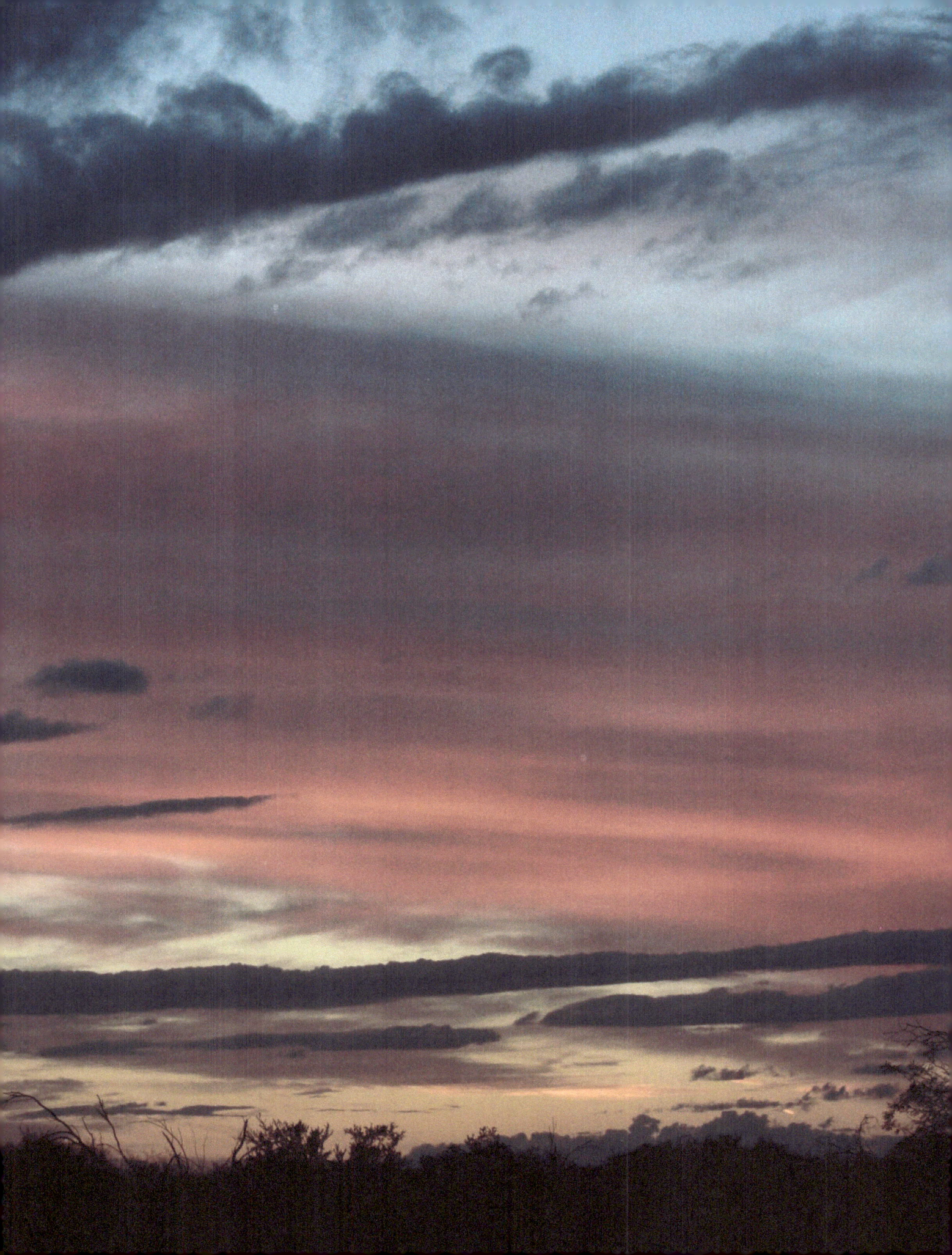

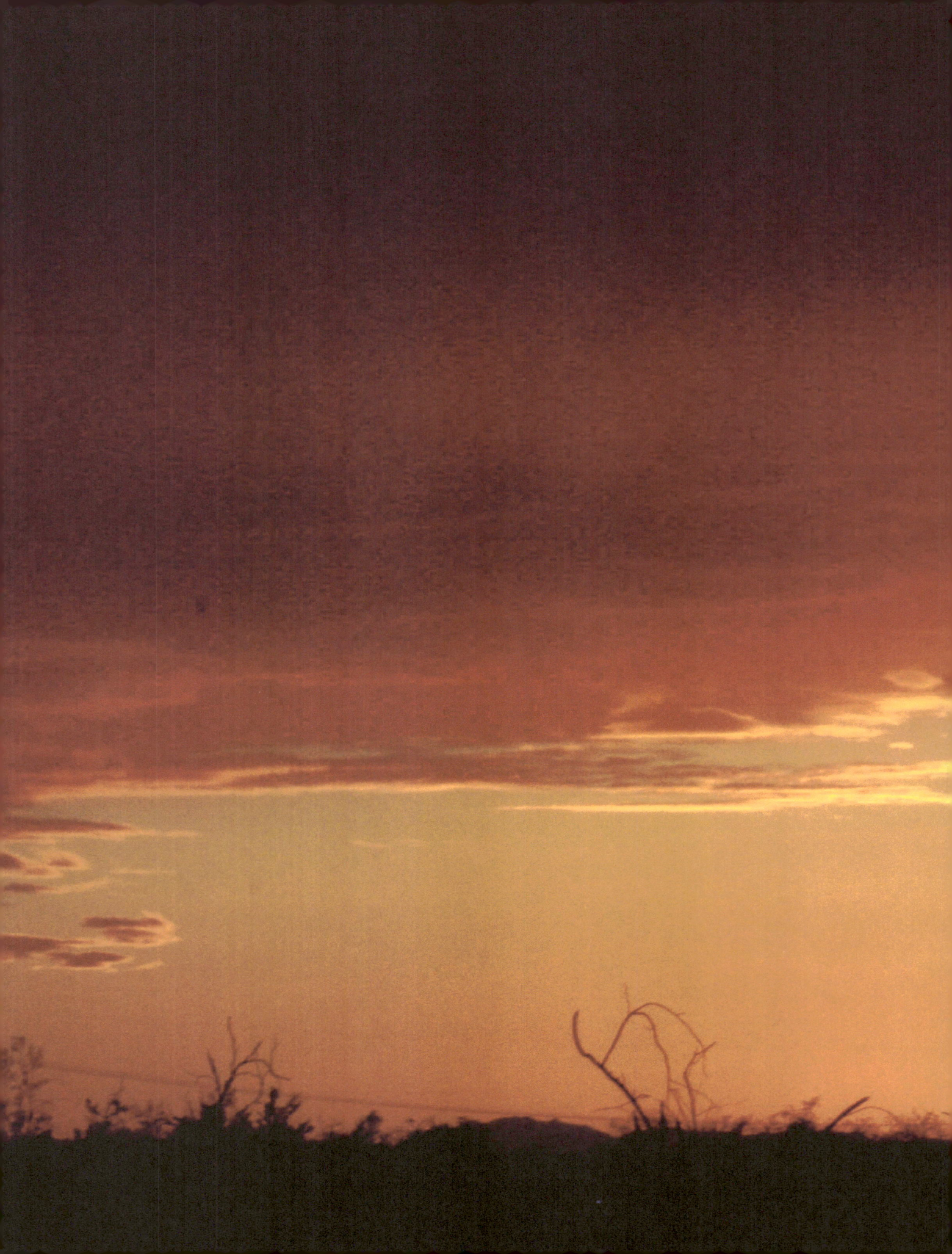

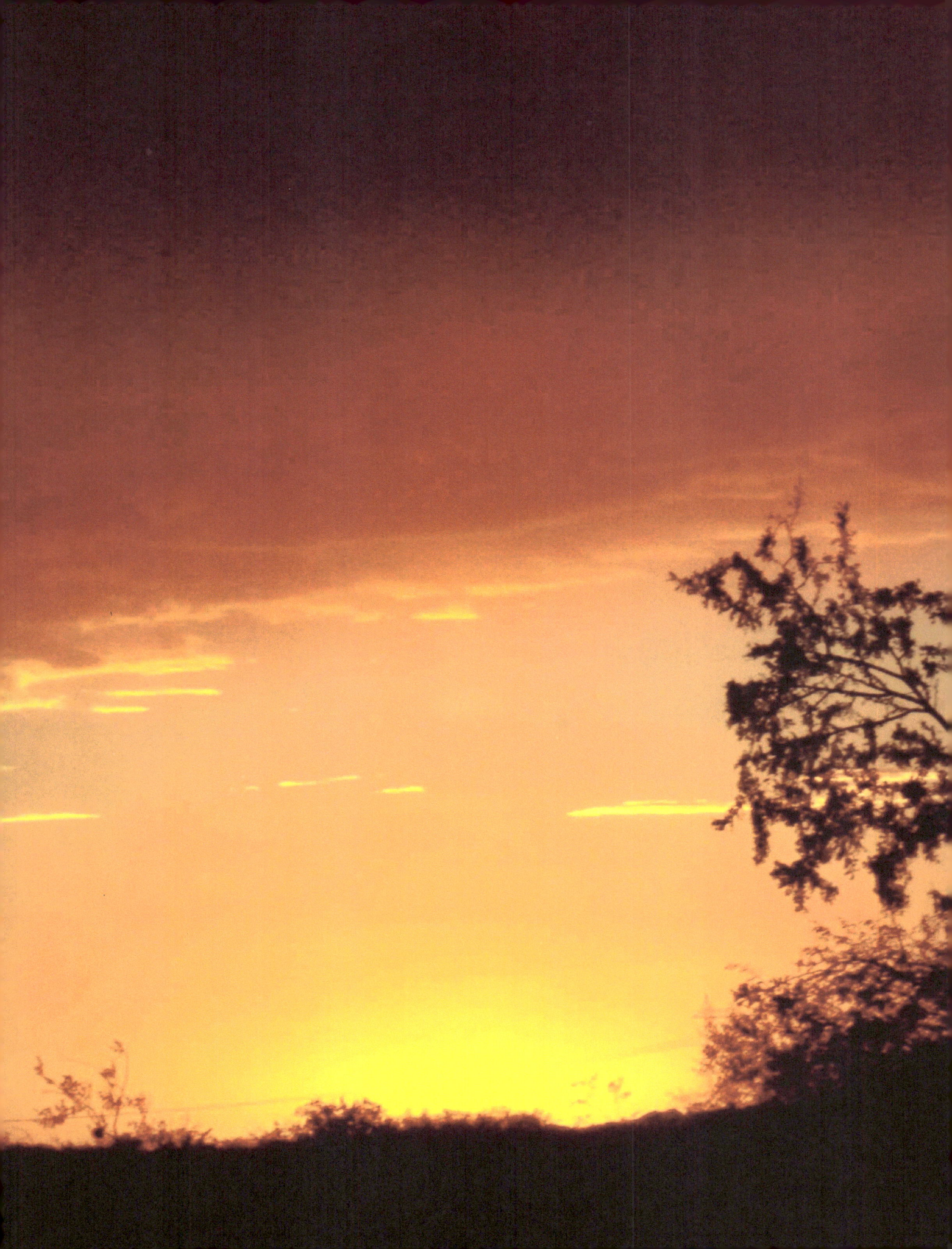

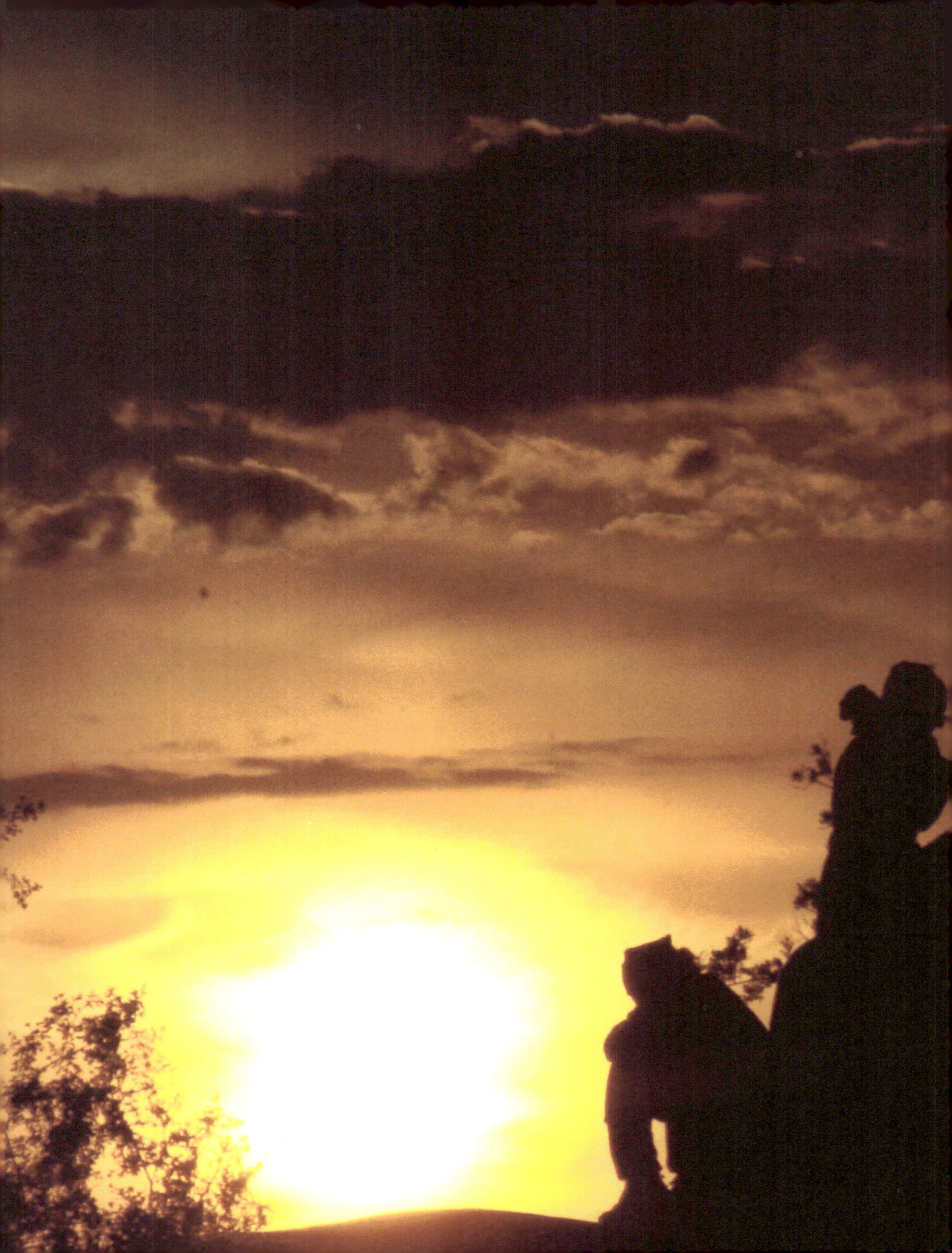

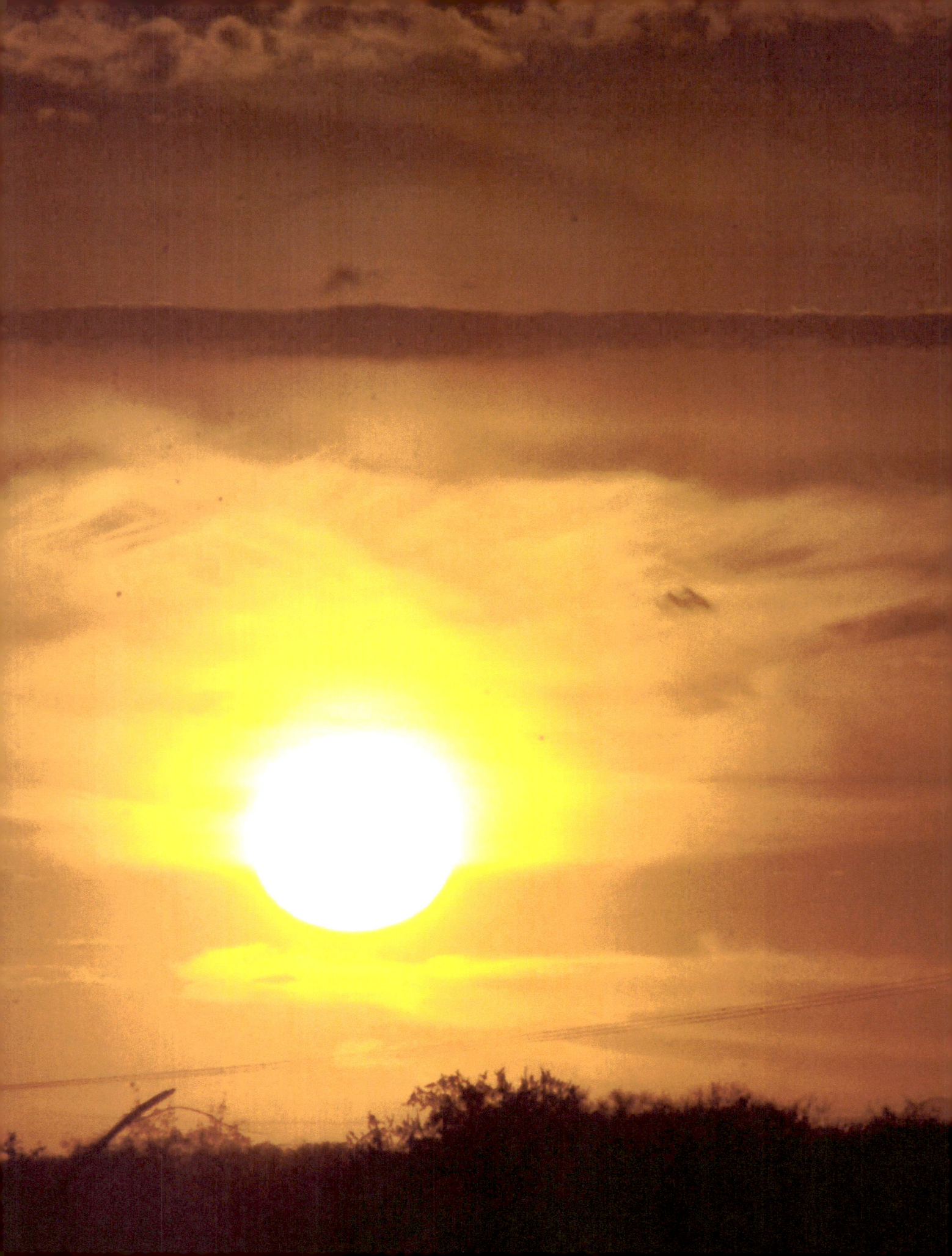

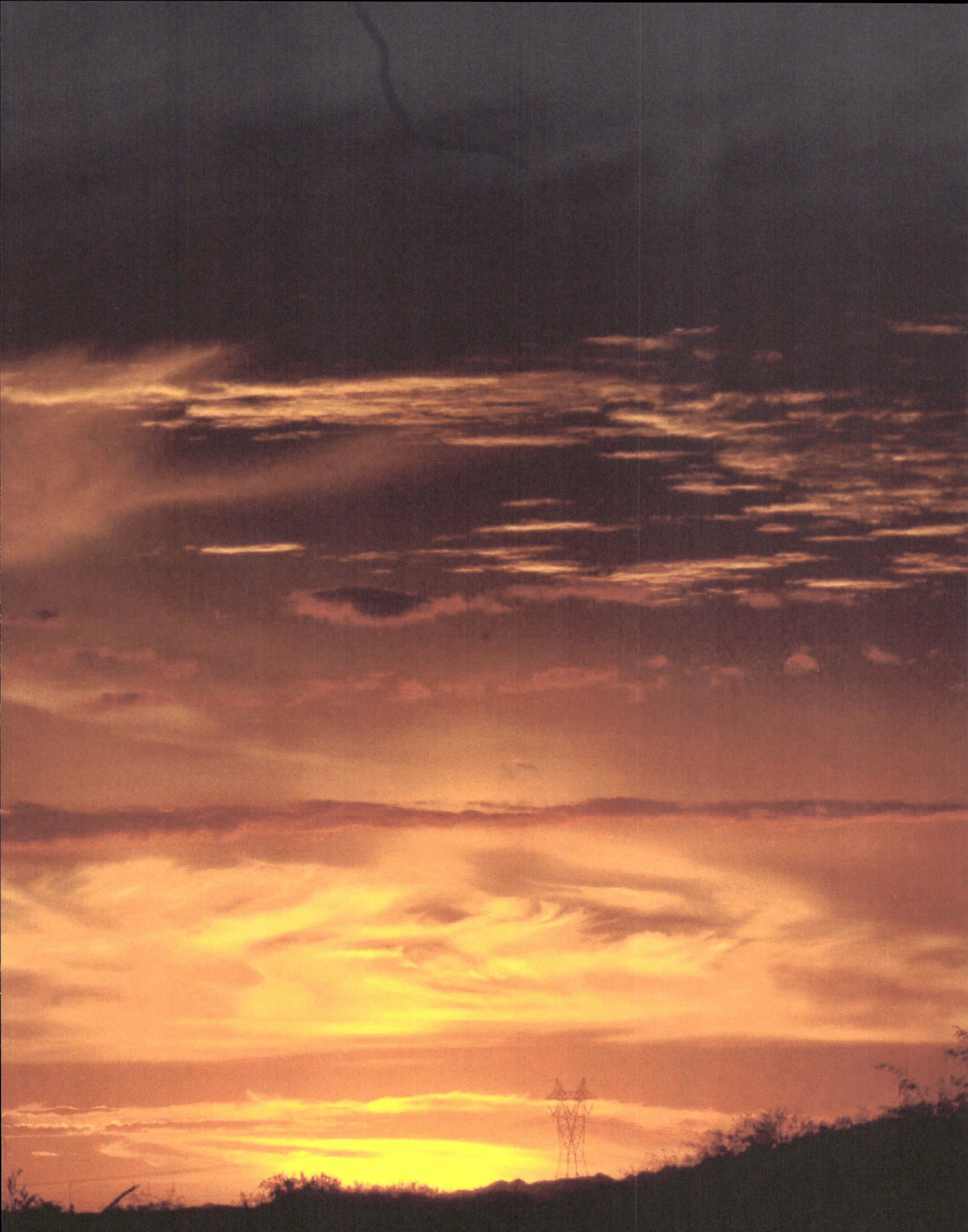

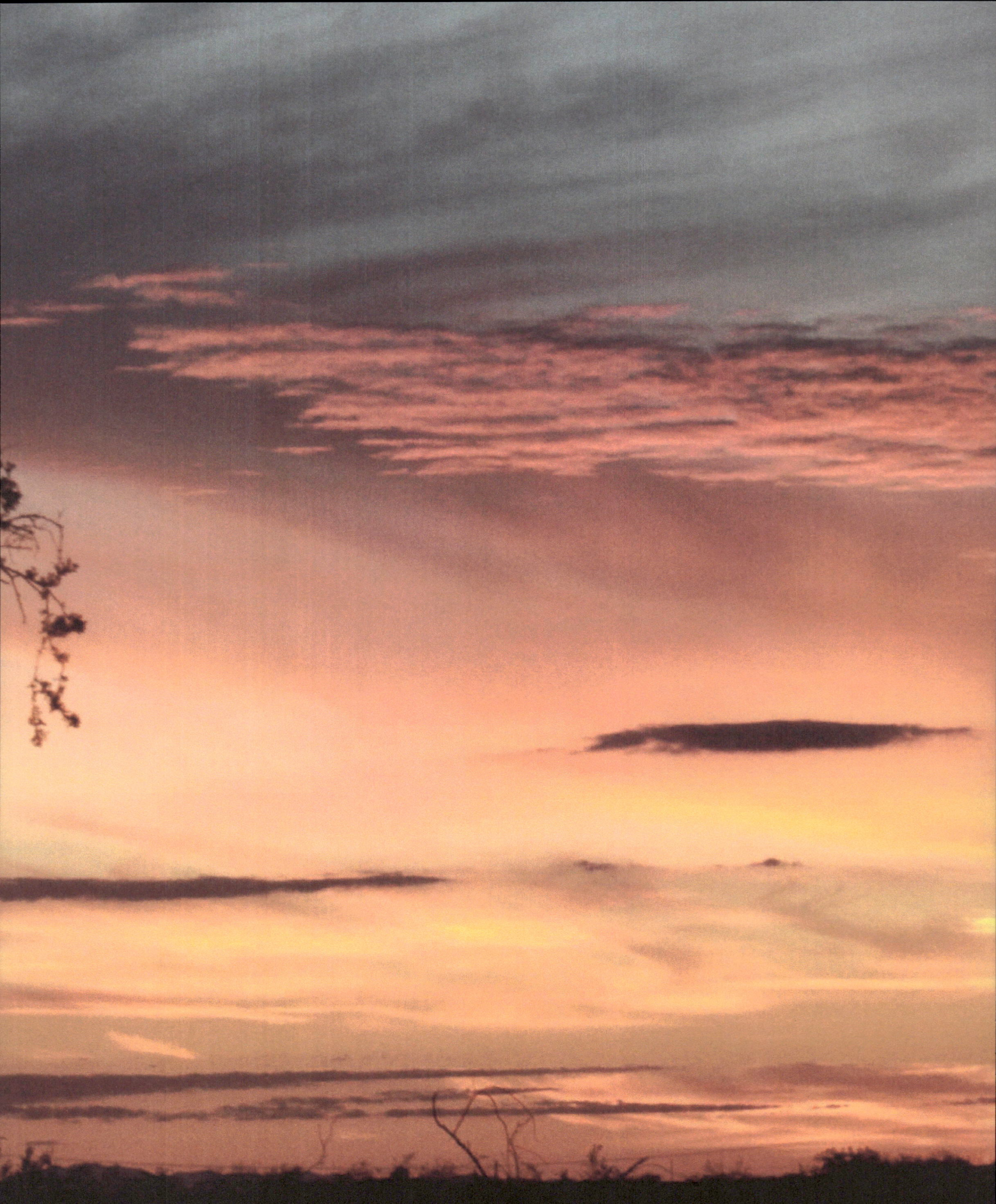

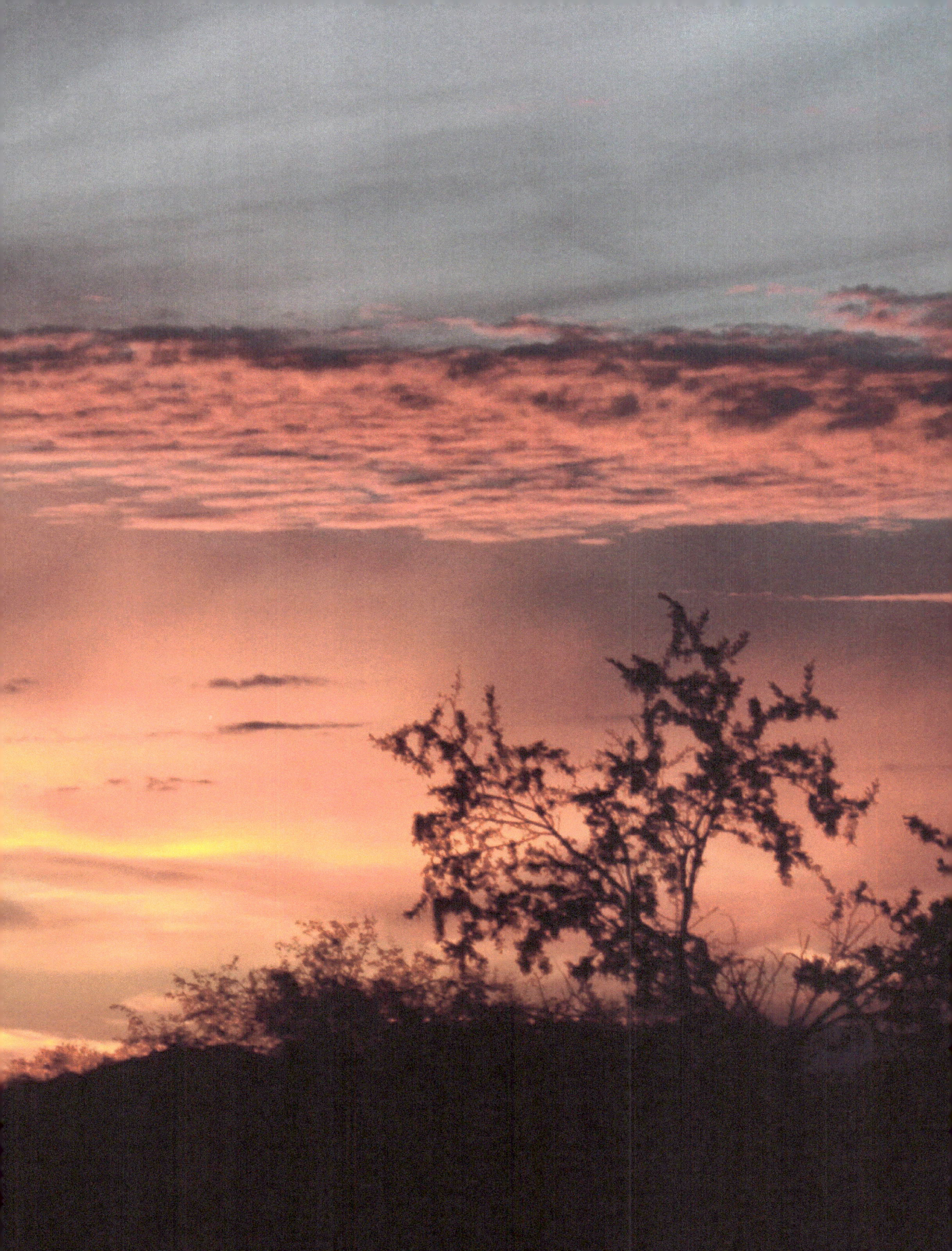

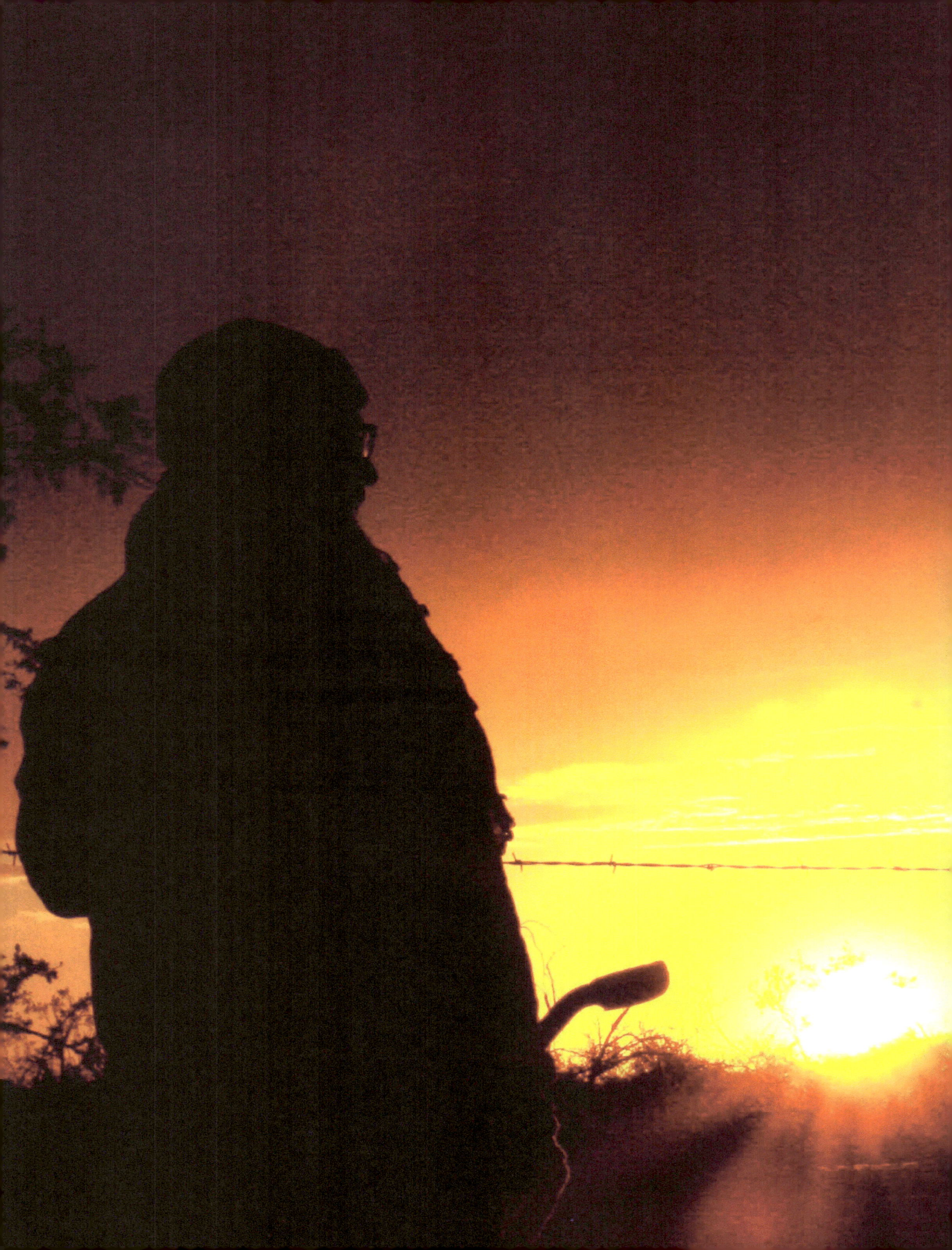

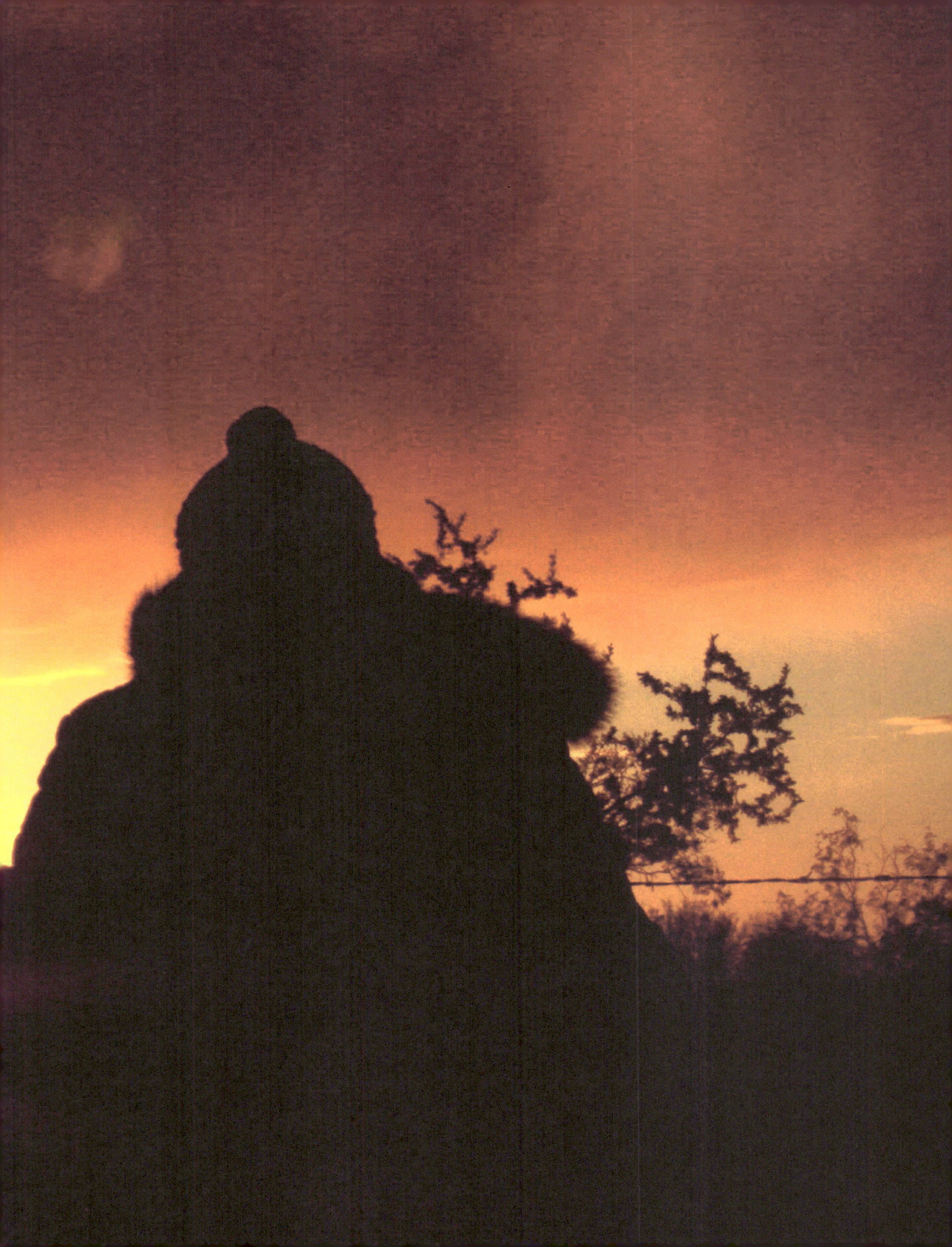